Enjoying embroidery

This book is dedicated to my husband Richard, our children, Vanessa and Bryan Graham; Simon and Alessandra Wilson; Susanna and Gavin Owen, and our grandson Alfred Owen

The material asserts itself through the hand.

Michelangelo

Enjoying Embroidery

Anna Wilson
Foreword by Constance Howard

Charles T Branford Company

© Anna Wilson 1975
Wilson, Anna
  Enjoying embroidery.
  Includes bibliographical references.
  1. Embroidery. I. Title
TT770.W53   746.4'4   74-32170
ISBN 0-8231-4032-6

Filmset by Servis Filmsetting Ltd, Manchester
Printed and bound in Great Britain by
The Pitman Press, Bath, Somerset
for the publishers
Charles T Branford Company
28 Union Street
Newton Centre
Massachusetts 02159

Contents

Acknowledgment

My affectionate thanks are given to all those students without whom this book could not have been written and also to those who have contributed to it by their work carried out in my classes and illustrated in the following pages.

My gratitude is offered to those whose books have been, and continue to be, so valuable to us all; in particular to Constance Howard, also Anne Butler, Kathleen Whyte, Edith John and several others.

I owe a special debt to a friend of many years' standing, Mary de Courcy Ireland, for her photography which enabled me to approach Batsfords with specimen material, and who is responsible for the photographs on pages 17, 18, 19, 29, 41, 42, 46, 53 and 68.

I must also thank Pret Singh for the photographs of Shirley Stewart's embroideries; David Finch for those of Vera Yates' work; Donald Davison for those of his wife's panel and above all, Terry Waddington, who has taken the great majority of these excellent photographs. In doing so he has treated me with charming patience and enabled me to illustrate the points I wish to make.

I am most grateful to a former student, Joan Haughton, for typing the script.

A W

C'an Quet, Deyá, Mallorca
Manchester, England 1975

Foreword

It is a pleasure to write this foreword to Anna Wilson's book which I feel will be of particular interest to all those who think they lack creativity. It is a visual record and proof that everyone has a talent even if it is undiscovered until the age of maturity is reached. It is never too late to find out.

I have known Anna Wilson since she was a student and remember her first appearance at Goldsmiths' School of Art as a hesitant embroiderer, almost sure that she would be incompetent and a failure. From her first piece of work which she describes so clearly, it was obvious that she had a natural affinity for choosing the right stitches and colours with which to carry out her ideas. Few students could do this. Her ability developed with her involvement, from the embroidering of simple household articles such as table mats, to the more complicated wall decorations that she now embroiders so successfully.

Anna Wilson has tackled more and more difficult problems of design and colour and discovered different ways in which to interpret these stitches. Her life now revolves around embroidery and her classes have become larger and more numerous as she has become known as an excellent and inspiring teacher, always encouraging and willing to take endless trouble with the beginner. Through her boundless energy, enthusiasm and high standards of achievement she has done a great deal to stimulate interest in embroidery as a creative medium. Undoubtedly she has given to many women in the north of England a new outlook and interest in life.

I hope that more study of a superb craft will have been sparked off after looking at this book. I cannot think of a better way of spending time than in working out original ideas in fabric and threads and Anna Wilson is doing an excellent job by fostering interest in this field.

Constance Howard 1975

Bibliography

Bibliography usually appears at the end of a book, but in this instance I think it is much more useful for it to be inserted at the beginning. All the books included here have been immensely helpful to me and to my students and should be read in detail and not just browsed through. I hope the ideas in this volume may inspire embroiderers working on their own to go back to the many excellent books which deal in greater depth with special facets of embroidery.

Inspiration for Embroidery Constance Howard Batsford, London: Branford, Newton Centre, Massachusetts
Simple Stitches Anne Butler Batsford, London: Praeger, New York (out of print)
Embroidery Stitches Barbara Snook Batsford, London: Crown, New York
Needleweaving Edith John Batsford, London: Branford, Newton Centre, Massachusetts
Creative Textile Craft, (Thread and Fabric) Rolf Hartung Batsford, London: Van Nostrand Reinhold, New York
Design in Embroidery Kathleen Whyte Batsford, London: Branford, Newton Centre, Massachusetts
The Stitchery Book Irene Preston Miller and Winifred Lubell Odhams, London

Embroidery Design Enid Mason Mills and Boon, London
Nature as Designer Bertel Bagor Warne, London and New York
Eye for Colour Bernat Klein Bernat Klein, Scotland with Collins, London
The Young Embroiderer Jan Beaney Kaye & Ward, London: Methuen, New York
Stitchery: Art and Craft Nik Krevitsky Van Nostrand Reinhold, New York
Introducing Patchwork Alice Timmins Batsford, London: Watson-Guptill, New York
Designing with String Mary Seyd Batsford, London: Watson-Guptill, New York

Introduction

I learned to embroider in my fifties as a part-time student under Constance Howard at Goldsmiths' College, School of Art. I arrived there in possession of a vocabulary of three inexpert stitches and was told to take a penny and make a design. I never stopped embroidering again.

After four years, my husband was moved to the North West, where I found little was known, outside the art schools, of creative embroidery and by this time my enthusiasm had become so unbounded that I was bursting to share it with housewives, like myself, who had no time or desire to do City and Guilds or Dip. AD examinations. This book is the result of a few years' attempt to help them to develop their talents. It is really my students who have written this book. I think I was lucky to begin my work in the North West where it seems to me that women, not surprisingly, have textiles in the blood.

However, most women find fabrics and threads exciting, they sew a little, and have a small vocabulary of stitches, so find it natural to use materials and threads as a creative medium.

In the last six years I have built up eight classes in further education under Manchester and Cheshire Education Authorities with over a hundred students and here I try to show how we begin to work.

Teaching aim

My first object is to infect students with my own enthusiasm and to see that they get pleasure out of their very first attempt.

It is often necessary to wean them from the boxes of multi-coloured stranded cotton which many of them bring to their first class, and to show them the innumerable possibilities in thread, ie, perlé, coton-à-broder, laine tapisserie, crewel wool, knitting wools, anchor soft, retors-à-broder, rug wool, strings, raffias, weaving yarns, strips of fabric (used as thread). See *Blue Moon* colour plate facing page 49. They must also learn a number of *line* stitches, *scribble* stitches and *texture* stitches and learn to design with these stitches. It is possible, even desirable, to start a student on a design with one stitch used imaginatively in a great variety of threads, while she practises the possibilities of other stitches on a small sampler.

In this way is learnt what different marks are made by one stitch by using different threads and when it comes to design, the student knows how to put the right mark in the right place.

Four samplers

We often make four samplers in some form of design and with some organisation of colour and texture. The benefit derived from acquiring practice in the grammar of embroidery can always be seen later in a student's work.

Of course, much is also learned in the context of panels worked in class under a teacher's guidance. I always have in mind the analogy between learning embroidery and learning a language and it is useful for direct and indirect method to go hand in hand.

It is best to work these samplers on hessian (burlap) or a similar weave and to keep to a modest size such as 30 cm × 46 cm (12 in. × 18 in.). As much as for a serious panel, a sampler should have an outline, 38 mm–50 mm ($1\frac{1}{2}$ in.–2 in.) from the edge of the fabric within which to arrange the design. I have repeated this deliberately later in the book.

Sampler 1 Line stitches

Prepare a small design by cutting a rectangle into various oblong and square shapes and arrange them as a skyline of buildings, outlining these with tacking cotton. Select a group of colours in varied threads. Decide on an organisation of colour, for example, darkest tones at base, growing lighter upwards, or darkest tones in centre, growing lighter to the outside, etc. Choose a suitable place for a focal point. Off-centre is best. This might be done in a touch of complementary colour. If the overall colour is green, this could be a red. In the diagram, 'F' might well be a good position.

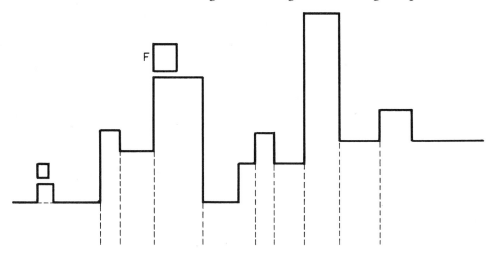

Line sampler by Gwyneth Jebson

A well-worked sampler in many tones of brown, mustard and yellow on natural material. A great variety of threads and line stitches. Decorative enough to grace a wall

Line sampler by M D Noblett
An attractive sampler in tones of blue, showing blocks of different stitches, ie, raised chain band, herringbone, eyelet holes, satin stitch, also groups of fine roumanian stitch

◀ *Line sampler* by Mary Duncan
A panel carried out in threads of varied thickness in tones of red and yellow. All in chain stitches (twisted chain, raised chain band, open chain) and couched lines of weaving yarn

Useful line stitches are:

(a) Chain stitches:
1 Open
2 Twisted
3 Whipped
4 Knotted cable chain
5 Raised chain band, etc

(b) Running stitch
This is a wonderful stitch for texture, for softening lines and for communication between one part of the design and another and for achieving a feeling of movement. See left: *Swarm of Bees* panel about 1·82 m × 1·21 m (6 ft × 4 ft) by Anna Wilson. This embroidery was worked for the Manchester Arts Festival June 1973, the bee being the emblem of Manchester Corporation and of the Festival. Now in the possession of Crowcroft Park School. Applied shapes of black and brown velvet, satin, gold lamé, gold kid. The net wings are embroidered with running stitch (darning) in perlé, coton-à-broder and single strands of stranded cotton.

(c) Stem
1 Portuguese knotted stem (a braid-like effect)
2 Raised stem band

(d) Couching
This may be done in a conventional, regular way or in a composite way.

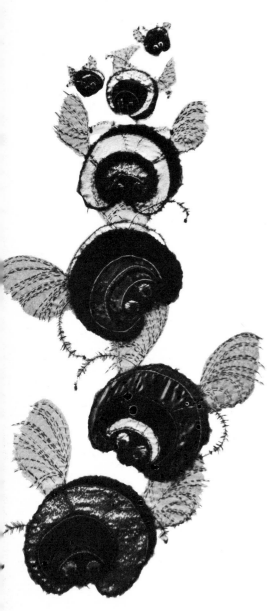

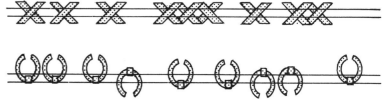

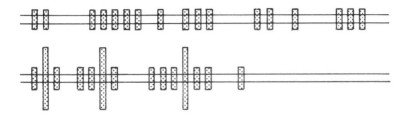

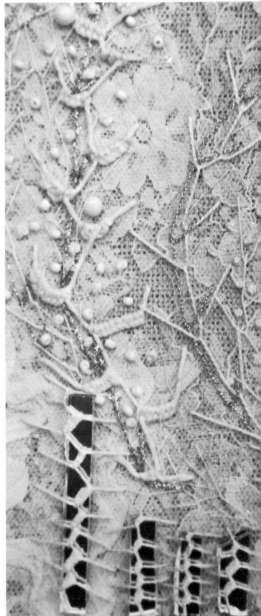

In the course of this sampler it will be seen how heavier texture can be achieved with a line such as that of knotted cable chain, how that line can be enlivened by carrying it out freely, ie, by not always completing the twisted chain base with the second surrounding chain. The effect of a stitch done in thick wool alongside the same stitch in one thread of stranded cotton shows how areas of contrast improve work. Equally interesting are contrasts of matt and shiny in the same colour.

In their efforts with a difficult stitch, students sometimes find they have created one of their own. See *Frost*, right.

Frost by Edith Robinson
Part of a panel worked entirely in white on a background of net and various laces. It shows a free scribble of feather stitches in perlé, coton-à-broder and retors-à-broder. The buttonholed feather stitch was arrived at accidentally by another student who was trying to do a composite feather stitch. It has been adopted by us all! The dark shapes are broken fragments of mirror glass applied by means of italian insertion stitch, freely executed. Reflections of this stitch in the glass add interest

Sampler 2 Scribble stitches

The first sampler is a somewhat ordered affair (though not unlively) of line stitchery and it is good to have a complete change by practising the use of cretan (up and down button-hole stitch). In order to loosen up, imagine you are embroidering a tangle of barbed wire. Such a sampler demonstrates the marvellous versatility of this stitch. It is easy to manipulate change of direction to effect contrasts by superimposing a line of cretan in one thread of stranded cotton, on, say, a cretan line of perlé (5 or 3). (See illustrations on pages 21 and 23.) Areas of more solid texture can be achieved by flower-like areas of cretan.

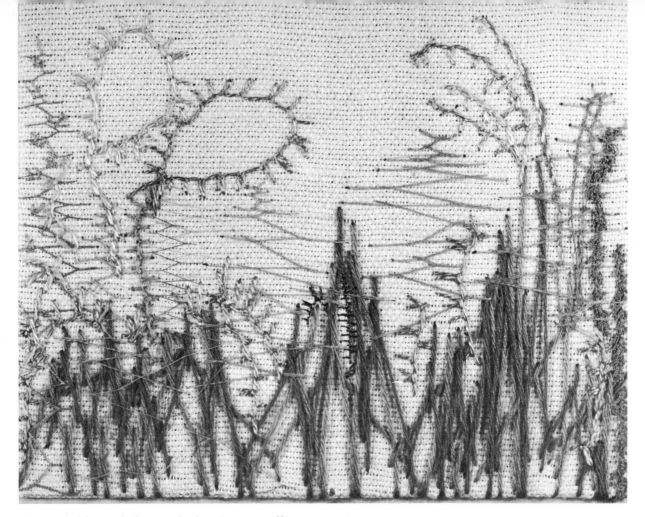

Cretan and buttonhole sampler by Anne Mullins
A scribble sampler in shades of pink. Thick wool, weaving yarn, perlé, coton-à-broder and single threads of stranded cotton have been used

◀ *Cretan and buttonhole sampler* by Anne Mullins
A more rigid use of cretan in two contrasting thicknesses of thread. The cretan stars are amusing. Could this have been inspired by fir trees in moonlight?

This scribble sampler could also be equally interesting carried out in feathery stitches, ie, Fern, Wheatear, Thorn, Single feather, Chained feather, Italian insertion.

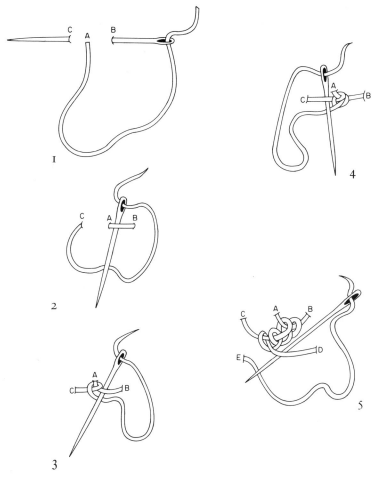

Italian Insertion

1 Bring needle through at A and insert at B, emerge at C

2 Make two surface buttonhole stitches on your bar A–B

3 In doing this you have made another bar from C–A

4 Take your needle over to the left and make 2 surface buttonhole stitches on C–A

5 Insert needle into fabric at D emerging at E. Continue as before on the bar made from your last buttonhole stitch to D

◀ *Cretan sampler* by M D Noblett
This shows excellent use of cretan to form flower-like areas. Surface cretan is also used in a lively variety of thick and thin threads

We often find ourselves inventing variations of these stitches. (See use of this stitch in Amy Richardson's *Exploded Circle*, opposite.)

Another good scribble stitch is fly (see *Areas of Scribble*, below).

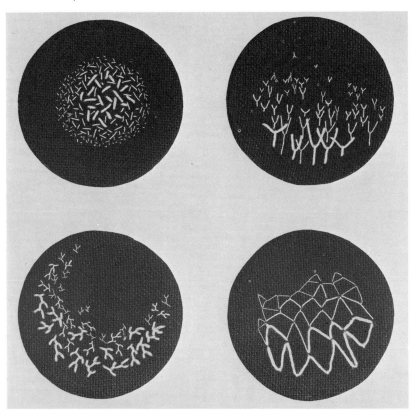

Areas of scribble by Anna Wilson

This sampler shows four possibilities of scribble ground-cover. It could be called four varieties of seeding, firstly orthodox, secondly with extended fly stitch, thirdly with sprigs of feather stitch and fourthly with fly stitch. All have been worked in retors-à-broder, coton-à-broder and one thread of stranded cotton

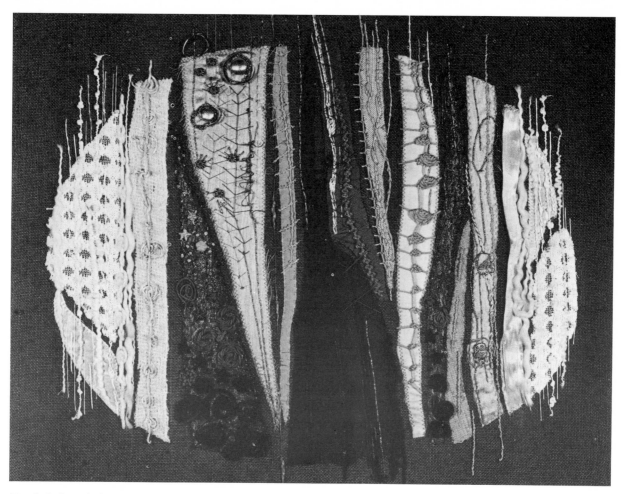

Exploded circle by Amy Richardson
A lively example of an exploded circle or oval. Interesting
fabrics and threads have been used. These range from browns
to copper, beige to cream. This student invents when she
does not know a stitch and gets fascinating results. An area
of interest (off-centre top left) has been created by some
pieces of copper. Italian insertion stitch has been built up
here to give a shell-like effect

Sampler 3   Free texture

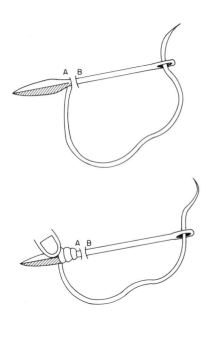

Imagine illustrating a diagram of geological strata. It is not necessary to know how to draw in order to outline with a tacked line on the background about four irregular curves (not wobbly lines). A template could also be made of a serpentine shape outlined on card and cut out. It could then be moved about to form varying curves and spaces in between.

There should now be four areas for stitchery. Again organise tone and texture. Thus area 1 might be a richly textured area of woven wheels, french knots, bullion knots, bullion loops, etc. Area 2 might be worked in irregular overlapping layers of buttonhole in slightly lighter weight but varied thread. In area 3 herringbone can be freely executed. And finally in area 4, a delicate free cretan in fine threads.

NB Sampler 3 can be made up into a successful cushion, edged with a handsome cord of one of the threads used.

Bullion Knots

It is a great advantage in making these to use a broad bladed, smallest size sacking needle (provided one is using a thread such as retors-à-broder, anchor soft, wool or raffia on a fairly coarse background. Take a tiny stitch of about two threads from B to A and push no further than the end of the broad part of the blade. Wind the thread gently (not too tightly) round the blade from the point A where it emerges, until you reach the length required. Pull the needle gently right through the loops at A and re-insert at B making an effect like a humped caterpillar.

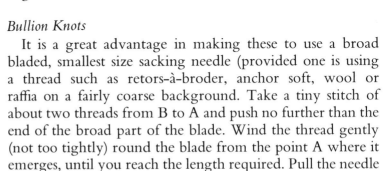

26

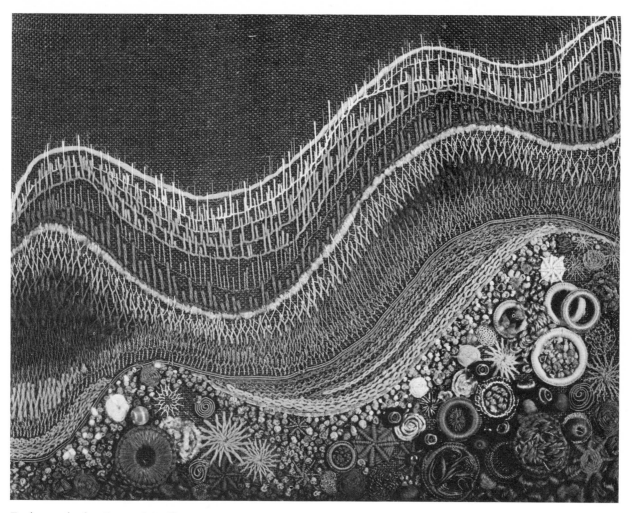

Red sampler by Joyce Muff

A good example of the geological strata idea. A rich piece of
stitchery carried out in all tones of red. The colour control is
excellent from deep, dull crimson to a tenuous, pale pink.
Heavy textured area of woven wheels, covered curtain
rings, knots and loops. Matt and shiny threads have been used
and it includes line, scribble and texture stitches

Sampler 4 Development of a simple shape with a limited number of stitches

For the last sampler, develop a circle, a squared circle or oval, of fabric with not more than three stitches, eg twisted chain, french knots and straight stitches. It is a useful exercise to do it in one colour. Liveliness must be achieved by use of matt and shiny, thick and thin threads. Arrange the fabric shape in the position preferred, remembering that the centre is very seldom the best place. The result of making four such samplers is to possess a small, private record of the most useful and versatile stitches in creative embroidery and quite possibly four small panels worthy of a place on the owner's wall.

Students should now be equipped to pass on to more ambitious designing and have developed an ability to put their vocabulary into practice and have acquired an eye for the beauty and infinite variety of the threads available today. Some students may even have acquired a touch of personal style, like handwriting.

Spring about 38 cm (15 in.) square by Joan Fern ▶
This lively sampler consists of a squared circle of staggered layers of white organdie on a lime green background. It has been developed in three stitches only; double knot, french knots and straight stitches, in a variety of white threads

Winter about 38 cm (15 in.) square by Carol Brown ▶
One of a series of four panels, representing the seasons. Carried out in black, grey and white, with a few pearls and silver knots. Straight stitches and a little needleweaving have been used

Fabrics and threads

Embroidery has a tactile quality and in achieving this the student soon realises the importance of fabric both for a background and for the shapes to be applied to that background. It is important therefore to choose a weave/texture that is sympathetic to the scale of the design.

A piece of wild silk does not form an easy background for the use of coarse threads like rug wool, anchor soft, etc (although small amounts might possibly be couched). There are many hessians (burlaps), furnishing fabrics, moygashels, etc which are excellent for large-scale, richly textured designs. Man-made fabrics such as bonded material are seldom interesting, and felt is only useful in small areas.

Dedicated embroiderers soon find themselves becoming unashamed magpies.

Fabrics should be collected in colour groups and kept together. (Polythene bags are excellent for the purpose.) It is essential to have a great variety – silk, cotton, tweed, satin, velvet, leather, etc.

Similarly, threads should be collected and kept in colour groups in transparent bags. Weaving yarns are invaluable for providing interesting lines and textures. Knitting wools grow more and more exciting and of course silks, cotton perlés, coton-à-broder, retors-à-broder, all sorts of string (marvellous variety of tone), leather thongs, raffia, etc, are useful. Students absolutely must set about forming a collection.

Textures by Mavis Lee

A gargantuan sampler about 92 cm × 61 cm (3 ft × 2 ft) worked in off-whites and beiges. It shows an interesting area of lively sheaf stitch, free raised stem band, blocks of lacy buttonhole, long, wrapped stitches, extremely elongated chain in one thread of stranded cotton, needleweaving

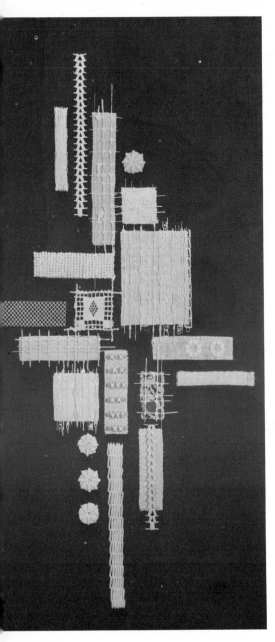

Of course, any keen teacher has a great variety of material and threads available in class, but she is not a prophet and cannot always foresee that the right thing is available on the spot. The time should come when each student has such a quantity and variety in her possession that it probably is only necessary to purchase two or three skeins of new threads for her current panel.

A good exercise is to glue scraps of material (in groups of harmonious colour) in as many variations of texture as possible, on to a small piece of hardboard.

It is interesting to consider also complementary textures, eg nets and hessian. Three-dimensional effects can be achieved in fabric by tucking, smocking, suffolk puffs, applying swathes of material etc (see illustrations, pages 35 to 39). Suffolk puffs are made by cutting out circles of fabric, turning in the edge about 10 mm ($\frac{3}{8}$ in.) and sewing it down with a running stitch to act as a draw string. When tightened and finished off it looks like a tam-o'-shanter on one side and a mob cap on the other. It may be applied either way up.

White sampler by Heather Stemp
A well worked sampler in all white on an emerald green background. Raised stem band, portuguese border, raised chain band, woven wheels, knotted cable chain, open chain. Long, large, white bugle beads have been couched in groups of cross stitch

Poppy by Rosa Bolchover (reproduced by courtesy of Dr Ian ▶ and Mrs Woolf)
A small piece of printed fabric enhanced by embroidery in twisted chain, double knot, french knots and beads

Page 33 *Sampler* by Elizabeth Wareham
A haphazard sampler but full of pleasant examples. Elegant contrasts in use of thread and interesting area on the right of italian insertion stitch used in wool, one thread of stranded cotton, anchor soft, raffia, etc

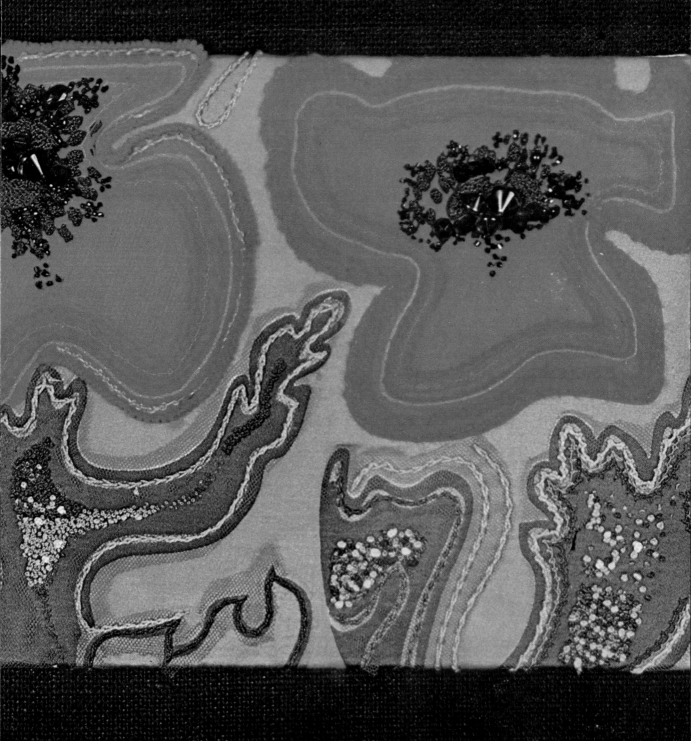

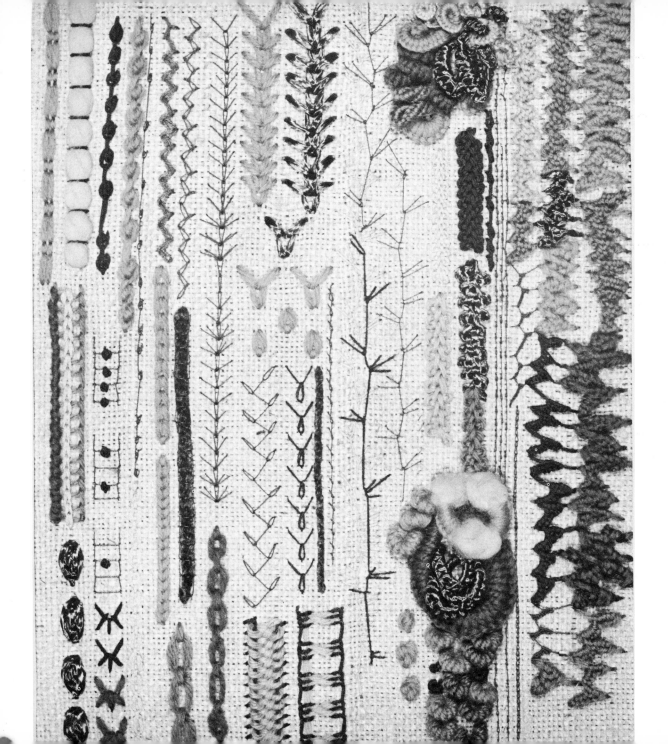

Sampler 1974 by Anna Wilson
A joke sampler consisting of little pillows of all sizes in tones of hot colour with a jade green one third from left in second row down. The woven wheel on the third pillow from right (bottom row) is also jade green. The pillows were embroidered before making up, in many of the stitches most useful in creative embroidery

Rocks by Winifred Bromiley
This exciting panel of strange shapes and textures shows the
use of tucked net, velvet, ribbed materials and rich stitchery.
It is in tones of yellow, ochre, cream and brown

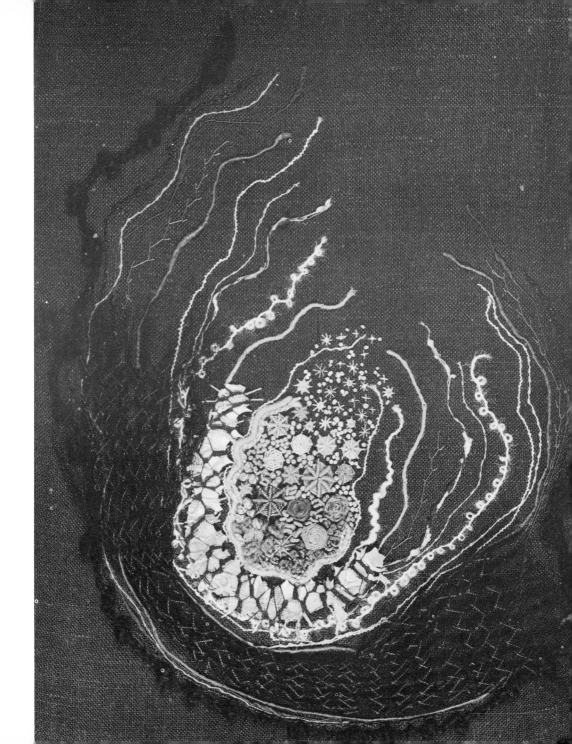

Pink abstract by Roberta Ann Parkin
A lively embroidery in shades of wine, petunia and pink.
Textures have been given special interest in use of several
suffolk puffs

◀ *Abelone* by Elsie Hartley
This embroidery in shades of navy, light navy, sludge,
mustards and cream was inspired by a crescent-shaped piece
of abelone. An interesting area of texture has been achieved
by the piece of pleated net with honeycomb smocking. The
abelone shape has been applied in needleweaving which gives
a mosaic-like effect

Yellow abstract by Margaret Lomax
Embroidery in browns, yellows and olive green. The three-dimensional central area of texture in this panel has been achieved by suffolk puffs and ruched circles of net. Card circles have also been covered with thread and used at varying angles. Much use of cretan

Capsicum by Anna Wilson
A sculptural embroidery on slate green hessian with swathes of black and bottle green net. Piled-up shapes of polystyrene covered in olive green hessian (burlap), ink-blue velvet, sludge mohair, a little dull gold lamé. Couched olive green weaving yarns, hand-made cords of green garden string. A coil of antique gold cord and a few gold beads give a point of interest. Design inspired by part of a photograph of a section of capsicum

Colour

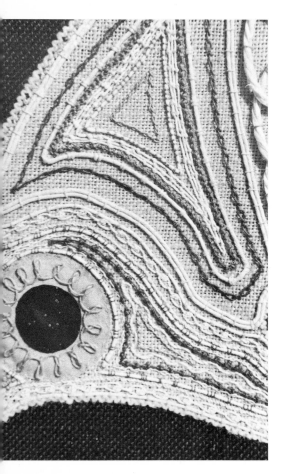

It is obvious that colour is an extraordinarily personal matter and one hesitates to say that it is a teacher's brief to inculcate Good Taste. The immediate reaction is to say 'It depends what you mean by good taste'.

It is amazing how little the average untrained person thinks about colour beyond choosing one that is becoming to her for clothes and naturally she also often reveals a certain deeply rooted preference in the decoration of her house.

I think it is helpful to make a fabric colour clock by outlining a circle on a polystyrene tile and then poking small strips of fabric into the twelve colour segments. They can be pushed in with a crochet hook and small dab of PVA adhesive.

Some students find subtle colour difficult and the eye has to be trained to discern it. The three primary colours, red, blue and yellow mixed, produce grey, but many tones can be in grey, depending on the proportion of the primary colour. There are blue-greys, brown-greys (when red is stronger) and marvellous – more or less – muddy mustards when yellow is added.

There are countless ways of observing colour. Try collecting a bag of different cords and strings. An embroidery worked entirely in strings is illustrated opposite.

Look at the colour in pebbles, stone walls, old roof tops, especially in the Mediterranean, tree bark, etc. Watch how light changes it all.

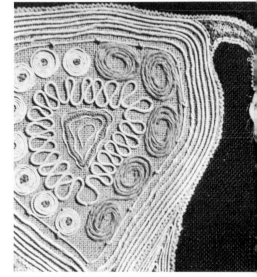

Bull by Heather Stemp
This panel has been carried out on an applied shape of natural on dark brown hessian. Horns and hooves of leather. Almost nothing but string has been used, thick, thin, from white to dark beige, from linen thread to sisal. Stitchery, mostly couching. Splendid areas of pattern

Right   *Bull* close-up of tail

Left   *Bull* close-up of eye

The lion of Alfabia by Anna Wilson
A decoration about 152 cm × 91 cm (5 ft × 3 ft 6 in.). This panel is worked almost entirely in strings. The applied shape of natural hessian is on a terracotta hand-dyed piece of uneven sacking. Hairy garden string, nylon string, linen thread, etc, have been used. Touches of shisha (indian mirror glass) and silver kid on mane and crown. Inspired by the coat of arms of an ancient family of the Mallorquin nobility. Edges have been allowed to fray freely

The lion of Alfabia
Close-up detail of head, mane and crown. The monocle-like eye of large, dull, steel beads

▶

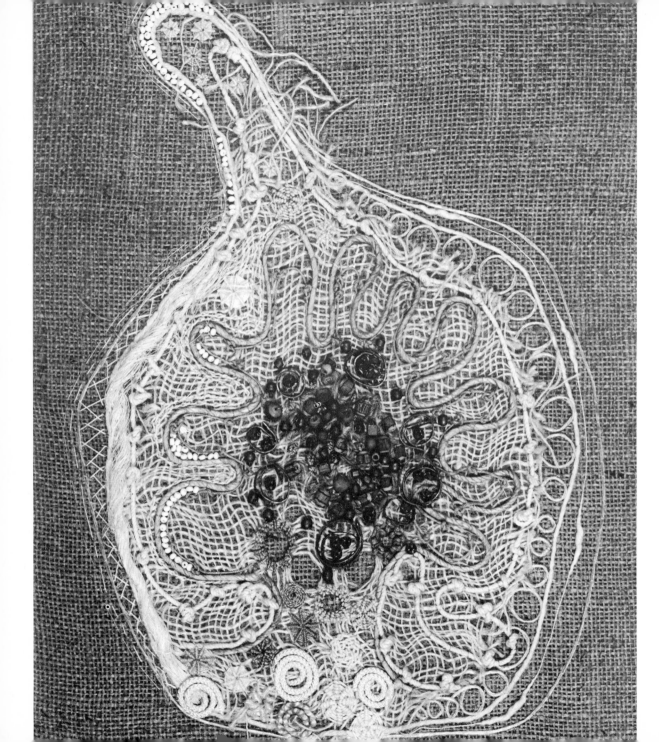

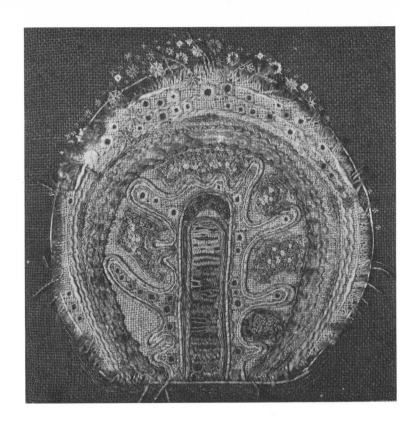

Cabbage 38 cm (15 in.) square by Anna Wilson
Inspired by cross-section of a cabbage. Much string has been used. Shape of natural hessian on red background. Central area of needleweaving, groups of eyelets, woven wheels and knots

◀ *Fig* 38 cm (15 in.) square by Anna Wilson
Inspired by cross-section of a green fig. Another embroidery carried out almost entirely in strings. Applied shape of coarse sacking on natural hessian. A few white china beads. Central texture of brown wooden beads and some coils of copper (painted with colourless nail varnish before applying)

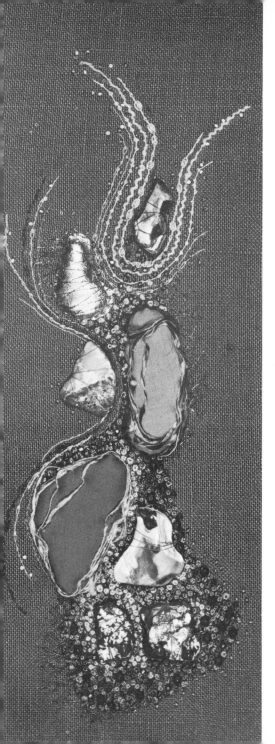

Many of the students have made designs to form a setting for pebbles in the way a jeweller designs for precious stones. The colour in the pebbles has dictated the scheme. Shells can be used instead of pebbles.

Setting for shells by Edith Robinson
Shells applied with invisible nylon thread. Soft tones of mauve and ochre in the shells inspired the colour scheme. Area of graduated french knots. Various weaving yarns form interesting lines

Setting for five flints by Anna Wilson (reproduced by courtesy of Mr & Mrs J Meier)
The extraordinary range of colour from cream to greys, browns and blacks in the flints inspired this colour scheme. Two shapes of foam covered in fabric and one in gold kid balance the outcrop of flints. A few miniscule grey and white beads have been used

Landscape is a wonderful source of subtle colour (see *Winter Landscape*, below). How much colour can be seen in a wet winter landscape – greys, silver, muddy mauves, burnt sienna, black, browns. (See *Wye Valley, Winter*, page 48.)

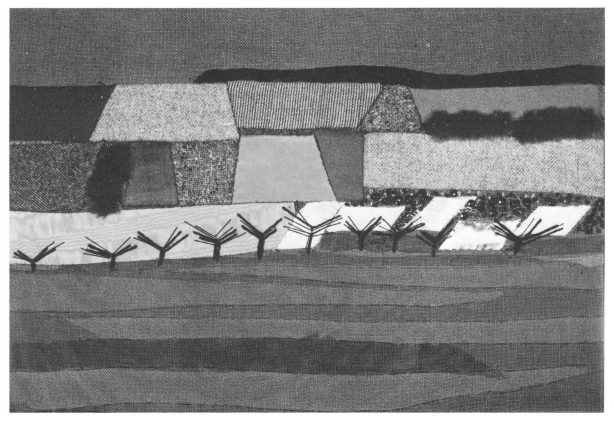

Winter landscape by Dorothy Wooding
An embroidery in tones of black, grey, silver and white. Interesting and surprising use of diaphanous net textures in foreground with substantial exciting pattern behind the trees. Areas of fur. How right fur can be as an abstract area of texture and how vulgar used realistically

Wye Valley, Winter by Anna Wilson
Inspired by a drive up the Wye Valley on a cold, dull March day. A leaden landscape of greys, silver, muddy mauves, burnt sienna, black and browns. Folded net, chiffon, etc, add to the texture. Point of interest in areas of silver kid, veiled by raised chain band. Open chain used for couching, knotted cable chain, woven wheels, straight stitches

Colour cards and swatches of material in a wide range are useful. Look at the pure colour of a child's set of building bricks (see *Poppy* facing page 32) the sugar-candy tints of sweet peas (see *Woman* facing page 81) or the shades in a rich Bernat Klein tweed (see *Circles* facing page 64). Try unravelling the threads of a good tweed. All these can produce colour schemes. Embroiderers are lucky to have a considerable amount of texture and colour ready made. Textures of stitches, changes in direction of stitches, can affect tone.

Design

Opposite
Blue Moon by Elizabeth Wareham
An interestingly designed sampler in subtle shades of blue
and silver on a very loose hessian background. Loops in small
strips of fabric, looped mohair, etc. Velvet and silver kid
have been applied, also an area of canvas work forming an
interesting controlled contrast to the other free texture. The
colour is well controlled

Work must give evidence of organisation. It must have a
wholeness and be arresting because it will be looked at across
a room, or from halfway; but when the viewer goes near to
it, the details of the texture (stitchery, etc) should give added
pleasure, and, to lovers and practitioners of embroidery, an
esoteric pleasure. A panel has to take shape within a given
area – most probably, but not inevitably, a rectangle. Students seem to find it extraordinarily difficult to remember
always to make a framework within which to arrange the
design. This should be a tacked line at least 38 mm–50 mm
($1\frac{1}{2}$ in.–2 in.) from the edge of the fabric, if it is to be stretched
over hardboard or a stretcher, or lined to make a hanging.

From beginning to end of the working of a panel it should
be constantly pinned up on a wall and the student should keep
getting back from it to see if the design works. Look at it
with half-closed eyes.

Design is always a pattern of shapes, but not a repetitive
one like a textile design. It is an arrangement of shapes to fit
into the chosen rectangle (or other shape). The shapes vary
in size and in direction. Thought is given to the negative
space as well as the positive space.

The design can begin anywhere in the given space. It can
be in the centre, off-centre, grow from the bottom or enter
from either side.

The panel must have a good focal point, or place of emphasis and by reason of the organisation of colours, line stitchery, etc, it will not detach itself from the whole design. This is why one must frequently hang work up on the wall to see that no area jumps out of its context. (Often an area of strong texture such as velvet does just this.) Try looking at it upside down. Does the design work better thus? Try looking at it in a looking-glass. Try looking at it on the floor. Even if a design is carefully planned one should be prepared to have to change it as it progresses if any area does not appear to work.

A member of one of my classes once said to me that as a post-graduate student social worker she was told that a diagnosis never ended until the case was closed. She rightly felt this applied to embroidery.

In non-vocational classes not many women are able to draw, though those who wish to do a figurative design can probably produce a stylised bird or animal. It is preferable, and often more instinctive, to cut or tear paper shapes quite freely. A circle of paper torn into pieces and spaced interestingly can be the basis of an abstract design and will make a student think about the nature of her medium more than something illustrative or figurative (see *Exploded Circle*, page 25). Nevertheless it is desirable to try and draw as much as possible in order to become more observant of the exciting shapes surrounding us and to be more selective in using them.

Seahorse detail of head
This shows the rich, crusty effect of the woven wheels

Seahorse by Vera Yates ▶
A lively embroidery for the quay-side cottage of yachting enthusiasts. It is carried out all in white with a touch of silver on navy fabric. Delicate background shape of net. Woven wheels of various threads. Perlé, silver Twilley, coton-à-broder, anchor soft, etc. Lively use of fern, wheatear and thorn

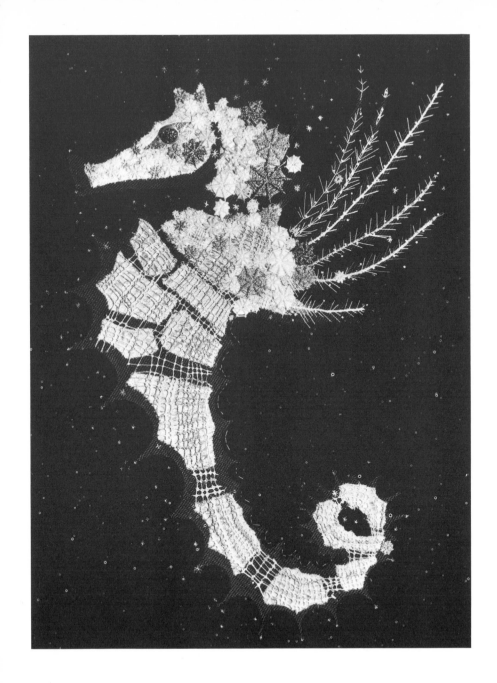

On the following pages there are more examples of work done in the classes. Like all the preceding ones they are the efforts of extremely busy women of different ages and standards of general education. I have been anxious not to draw on the work of the professionals, or the embryonic professionals in the art-schools. This book is about amateurs. I have attempted to describe the photographs fully, so that the reader can visualise them. They should be looked at in the critical way one scrutinises embroideries in an exhibition. It is a sad fact that, however objective the student, or however analytical the teacher may be in class, in retrospect one often perceives errors or omissions. Luckily the layman's pleasure in an embroidery possessed or viewed is seldom so carping. Nevertheless, it is a valuable exercise to use one's critical faculties in this section. For this reason, I have, in a few captions, put forward questions which may be considered rhetorical or not, as the reader wishes.

When I came to consider which panels would best illustrate my subject of samplers and which would pursue our work into wider fields of creativity, I realized how attached many people seem to be to trees and landscape. The following group of embroideries inspired by these two subjects show how personal are the statements made by the students about them.

White garden by Winifred Bromiley
A dreamlike, imaginative embroidery all in white on a
blue-grey background

Trees by Pru Barron
A more robust embroidery than the last (approx 91 cm–3 ft
square) but romantic enough to be a setting for the Babes in
the Wood. Interesting textures, an area of rya, knotted strips
of fabric, frayed material, free needleweaving in the trunk
of the tree on the right. Fern stitch, cretan and italian insertion stitch have been used. Worked in browns, greys,
beiges and creams on natural hessian

◀ *Trees* by Pru Barron
A lyrical piece of work in a well-controlled organisation of
off-whites. Good use of Edwardian laces, crochet motifs,
embroidered net and plain net. A touch of cretan has been
used in the sky. Also an interesting group of sheaf stitch,
used like seeding (see also illustration page 24). A line of
portuguese stem stitch makes a cord-like effect

55

Summer by Margaret Leigh
One of four roundels of trees, representing the seasons. Branches suggested in needleweaving. The student has drawn threads from the fabric used in foreground and couched them to give texture. A few touches of tête de bœuf in pinks round tree. Shades of green on navy background. Roundel surrounded by a couched weaving yarn

◀ *Waterfall* by Pru Barron
Another romantic panel. Good use of exciting fabrics. Folded black net has been used to form an attractive shape

Autumn tree by Lilian Benbow
Background of four tones of lace from browns to palest coral. Twisted chain and knotted cable chain give texture to trunk and branches

Cornfield by Anne Mullins ▶
This embroidery is done entirely in yellow. There are lines of italian and trapunto quilting. A few gold beads between the padded shapes. Tufting. A little cretan. A very interesting combination of machine and hand embroidery. Do you prefer this design with the lines seen vertically?

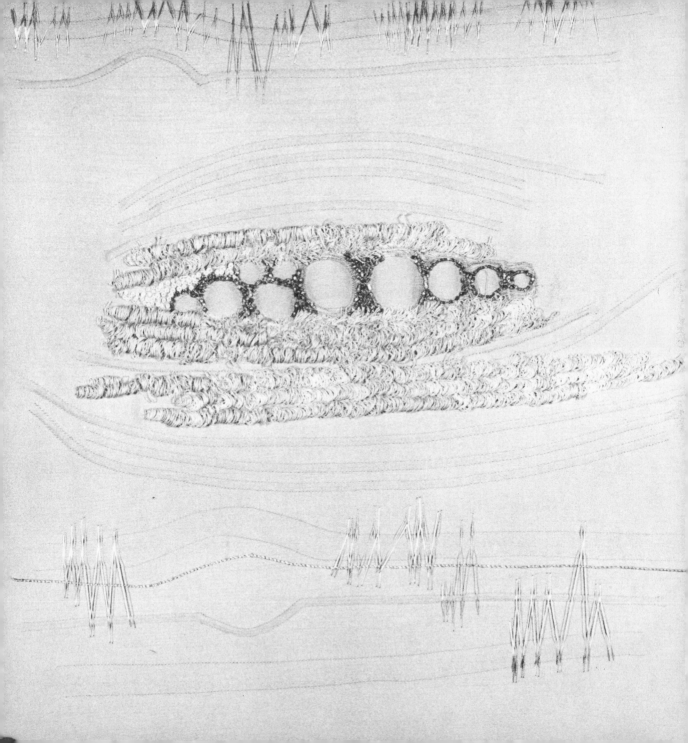

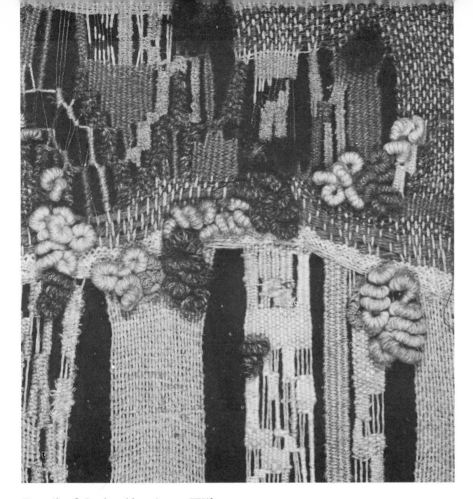

Detail of *Orchard* by Anna Wilson
This panel is almost entirely worked in needleweaving in a
great variety of string, yarns, mohair, wools, etc. Groups of
bullion loops worked with small sacking needle as shown on
page 26. Can it truly be called an embroidery?

◀ *Lime* by Lilian Benbow
A well drawn tree. Developed contours in needleweaving
with varied threads. Delicate branches a good contrast to
solid trunk. Do you consider the embroidery gives the panel
a special quality which redeems its realism?

Pennine Valley at night about 36 cm × 25 cm (14 in. × 10 in.)
by Anna Wilson
Foreground of tucked net, cord, braid, a rouleau of velvet in
deep dull red, browns, muddy mauves, fawn. Large square
sequins applied with raised chain band in varied thicknesses
of thread. A 'seeding' of extended fly stitch (see illustration
page 24) and a few gold beads

◀ *Evening road* by Anne Mullins
A large panel about 91 cm × 61 cm (3 ft × 2 ft) on a coral
background with trees of patterned black fabric and road-
way of tucked beige net. Lines of weaving yarns and groups
of stitches, fly, detached chain, raised chain band, herringbone, running stitches

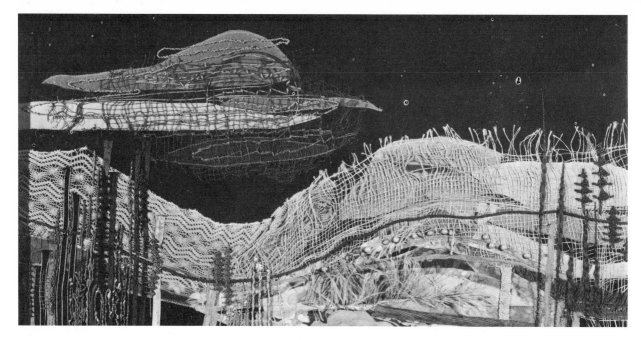

Landscape by moonlight by Shirley Stewart
A bold imaginative panel worked on a black background. A copper ring suggests a moon. Exciting fabrics have been included – an old piece of knitted stocking, onion bag, loose weave sacking, an ostrich feather, a few wooden beads, etc. Some spiky areas of italian insertion (see diagram page 23) on the right show what a creative stitch this can be

Page 65 *Reflection* by Marian Mullineaux
A tender piece of work in very soft blues and grey-greens. Many different weaving yarns give ripple effect

Circles about 76 cm × 46 cm (2 ft 6 in. × 18 in.) by Anna Wilson (reproduced by courtesy of Mr & Mrs Max Milner) A design based on cirlces. The colour scheme was inspired by a small piece of Liberty Varuna wool, used for one of the circles. Embroidery mostly woven wheels

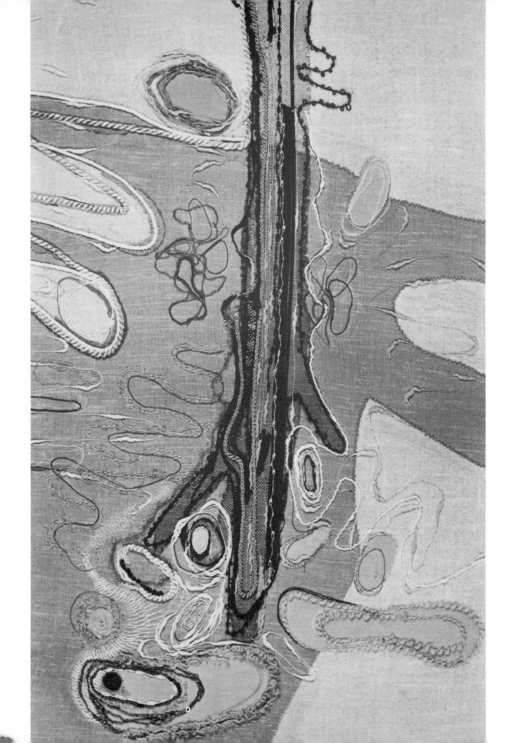

Birches and beeches about 122 cm × 61 cm (4 ft × 2 ft) by Ivy Rogers
A hanging in needleweaving, in a great range of very soft greens and greys. Wools, anchor soft, perlé, etc, have been used, also a few hand-made grey-green beads. The background has stripes of soft beiges. Do they disturb a little?

Mallorquin landscape by Vera Yates
A sense of impending storm hangs over this embroidery. Colour in the net background has been carefully organised, to which the dark silhouettes of the windmills and the pine branch are a good foil. Although totally realistic, this panel also has a quality only embroidery can give it.

Needleweaving can provide an excellent encouragement for conventional inhibited embroiderers to loosen up. One can improvise continually

67

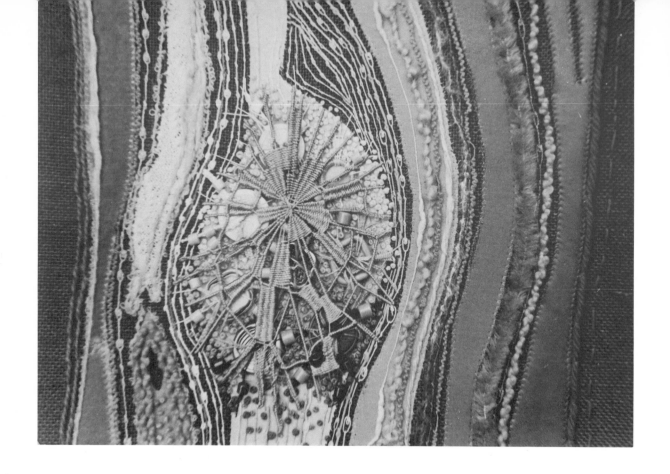

Detail of *Bark* by Heather Stemp
A good area of needleweaving which forms the focal point of a panel based on a drawing of a piece of bark. The embroidery was carried out in reds, oranges and yellows. Interesting yarns, including fun-fur can be seen

Trees by Edel Zollinger ►
Another group of trees in shades of green in which there are some exciting tufting and bullion loops. Small padded shapes at the base.

Is the fabric in which the trees are enclosed of too strong a pattern?

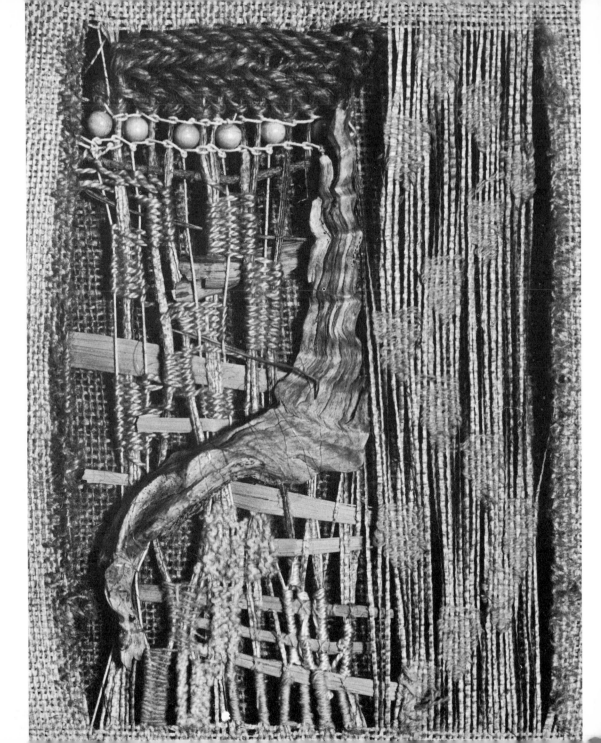

Skeleton 23 cm (9 in.) square by Anna Wilson
One of a series of four fig leaves representing all the seasons.
Background shape of black net on scrim. Built-up layers of
needleweaving from thick to very fine, black to grey. A
small shape of silver kid, top left and three cut-outs of silver
sequin-waste. A few Edwardian jet and steel beads give it
interest

◀ *Needleweaving sampler* by Charlotte Quail
An interesting rectangle of needleweaving showing great
contrasts; solid on left with lovely piece of olive wood and
bits of dried palm; delicate area on right woven slightly with
threads that have been withdrawn

Flowerhead detail of centre
Woven wheels, buttons, beads,
french knots give
three-dimensional effect

72

Rain about 122 cm × 61 cm (4 ft × 2 ft) by Anne Mullins
A very large panel. The background is grey with applied rifts in varied fabrics in blues, greys, olive greens, with mostly machine stitching. The three rather sculptural figures (from left to right) are in tones of grey, olive and dark blue. The umbrellas are in three versions of the same striped print. Stitchery on the figures mostly raised chain band and knotted cable chain. Some french knots and running stitch. A sparkle has been given by use of interesting faceted gun-metal and iridescent blue-black beads

◀ *Flowerhead* by Audrey Davison
This design has been worked on a blue background in shades of blue-green. The top right hand petal is lime, giving a focal point. The centre is richly textured. The colour in it relates to that of the petals

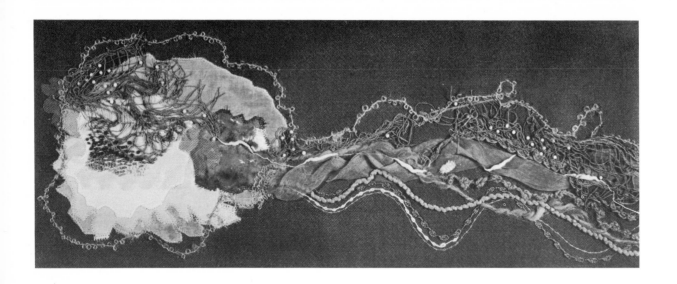

Blue and green panel by Pru Barron
This embroidery has a background of midnight blue. Looped mohair and other interesting yarns couched on. A twist of organdie, chiffon and pieces of onion bag have been used. A focal point bottom left of lime green and hyacinth blue with french knots in tones of darker greens

Left *Poppyhead* by Constance Murphy
A panel in browns and string colours on natural hessian (burlap). Woven wheels provide texture. Line stitches mostly twisted chain and knotted cable chain. One or two hand-made cords

Candles about 106 cm (3 ft 6 in.) square by Anne Mullins
A large embroidery in delicate tones of greys, apricots and
creams. Two flames of gold kid. Strong bold stitchery.
Reverse chain, built-up thickly, gives interest to three flames.
Tweed shapes have been deliberately frayed

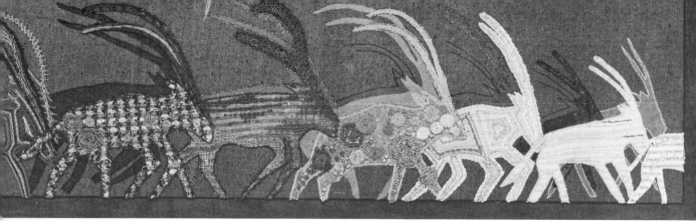

Stampede by Constance Murphy
A decorative panel on rust coloured bark cloth. Good pattern achieved in horns

Pavements by Constance Murphy
This embroidery was based on a photograph of an area paved in fan-shapes of pebbles, stones, etc. Rich browns and coppers have been used

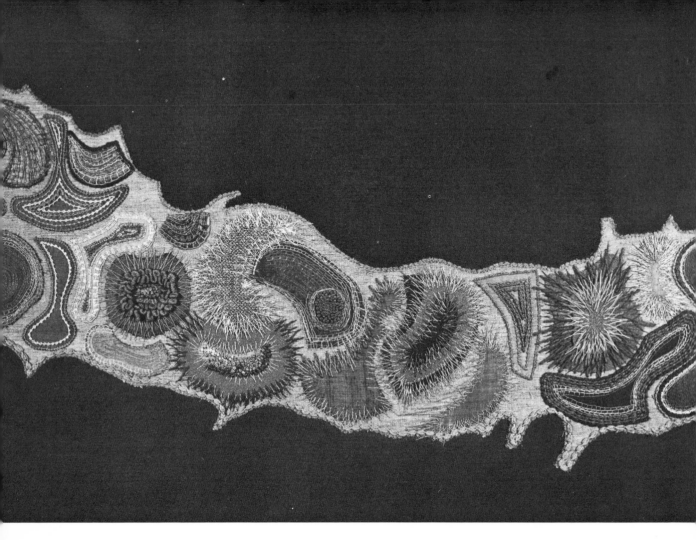

Purple and green panel by Patricia Dunkin
A beautifully stitched panel. This student has a great predilec-
tion for open chain which she uses well. Also cretan, double
knot, bullion loops and knotted cable chain have been used

Patchwork hanging by Midge Braddick ▶
An enterprising piece of work, as this student has also made
the ceramic pendants. These pick up the soft mauves, reds
and blues of the patchwork

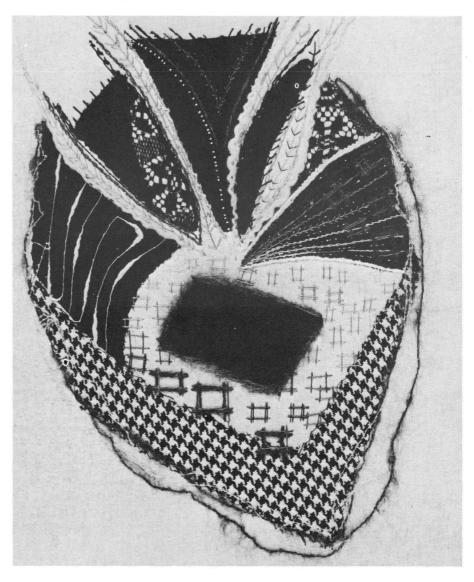

Black and white abstract by Winifred Bromiley
This design was inspired by the boomerang shape of check
tweed. Touches of dark grey mohair

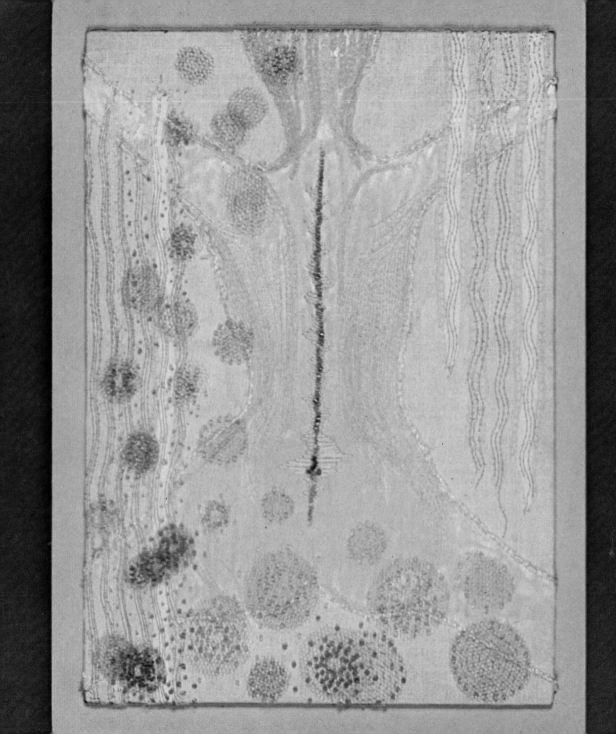

Noah's Ark by Rosa Bolchover (reproduced by kind permission of Joanna Woolf)
A charming nursery embroidery. Amusing choice of animals

Woman about 254 mm × 178 mm (10 in. × 7 in.) by Ivy Rogers
Tiny one-thread twisted chain in areas. Bubbles of minute pink and blue beads. Delicate ripples of water

81

Fish by Ivy Rogers
Worked on a blue ground of furnishing fabric – a piece of old silver tights and frayed pieces of silk have been applied. Interesting scale-like beads have been removed from an evening dress and sewn round the eye

Abstract by Patricia Dunkin
Applied shape tie-dyed in rich browns, dull reds and muddy
orange by the student. Embroidery worked on a background
of very dark plum-coloured hessian in shades of dark brown,
dull reds and muddy pink, burnt orange to pure orange in
focal area. Areas of open chain, couched threads and innumerable woven wheels

Estuary by Joan Brandon
A rich sampler of stitchery in pastel colours, giving a feeling of tides and eddies. Innumerable different stitches may be discerned in it

Summer meadow about 30 cm (12 in.) square by Sheila Bennett ▶
An experiment using small scraps of a Liberty silk in black, coral pink, powder blue and cream. Shapes have been applied to a scrim background and embroidered in these colours. The roundel has been padded

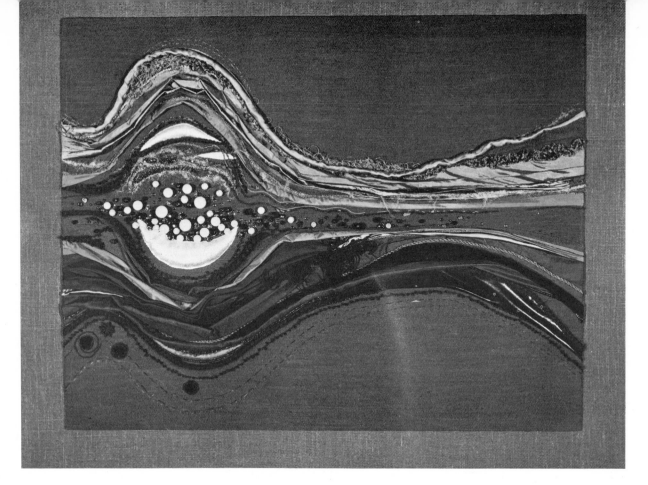

Moon river about 122 cm × 76 cm (4 ft × 2 ft 6 in.) by Edel Zollinger
A very large embroidery worked on a navy background. Folds of velvet, satin etc from black, navy, light navy to greys and silver. Good contrasts of fabric. Some interesting pale grey beads in focal area

Blue cross by Edel Zollinger
A panel in deep blues and rich reds. The velvet square is mounted on board, the inner shape of satin is padded, the embroidery on it having been worked first

▶

Abstract by Shirley Stewart
A panel in hot colour. Interesting use of lampshade bobble
and other fringes. Buttons, covered curtain rings and woven
wheels give texture

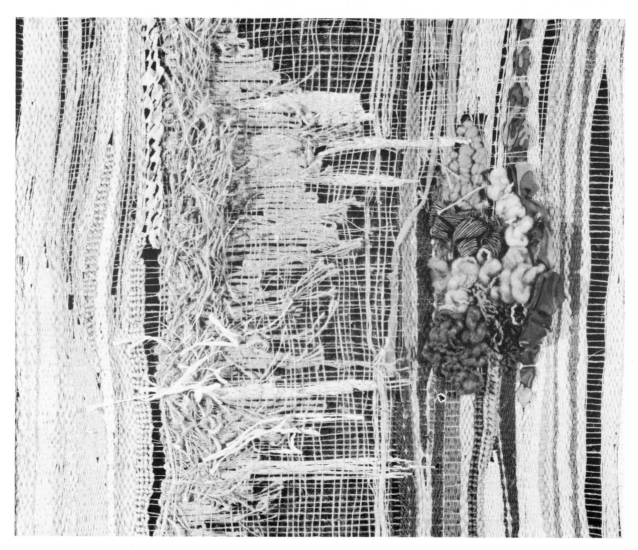

Detail of *Abstract* by Shirley Stewart
Worked on a very loose jute fabric. Threads have been
pushed to form interesting spacing and in some areas closely
woven. All in off-whites except for dramatic focal point of
hot colours

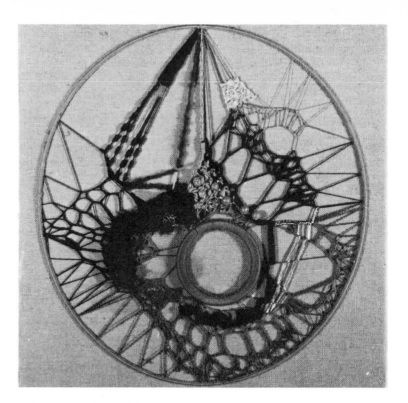

Woven wheel by Shirley Stewart
Such a wheel can be mounted on a fabric covered board, or left to hang freely as a mobile. The 56 cm (22 in.) lampshade ring is first varnished with colourless lacquer (so that the wheel may be washed without fear of rust) and then button-holed all round with wool. The central ring is anchored to the edge with various threads which act as a warp and the whole has been built up quite spontaneously with needle-weaving, loops, beads, etc

Pineapple by Vera Yates ▶
This was a beginner's piece of work in very rich colour and proved a robust effort. The built-up reverse chain in the leaves is effective. The sections of the pineapple are padded

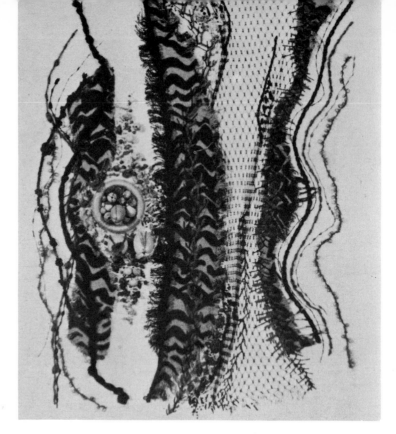

Abstract by Marion Grant
This was a first effort by a complete novice, with very little
guidance, except in stitchery. It was inspired by the scraps of
striped material. A sensitive feeling for fabric, thread and
texture was at once evident

Menora about 122 cm (4 ft) square by Agneta Levi ▶
A large panel in the possession of the Menora Synagogue,
Cheshire Reform Congregation. This student dyed many of
her threads and wools to achieve a great range of browns,
blacks and copper. The focal point is a flame-shaped piece
of copper sheeting. The shapes are padded and three-dimensional. Shadow effect obtained by use of net

Epilogue

One only learns by working, and a lively class is the best stimulant. Members of a good class spark off each other. It is extremely important not to over-direct. Once a student acquires sufficient technique to make the marks she requires she will develop a style and I always find her work becomes extraordinarily like herself – it may be coolly intellectual, romantic, nebulous, vulgar (and why not?).

In embroidery one is not mixing paint or trying to copy a painting, but endeavouring to make a personal statement that one feels is best achieved in fabric and thread. We hold humble, but frequent exhibitions ourselves. I insist that students go to all the available exhibitions (not only of embroidery) in our area and we try to keep abreast of aesthetic climate.

Suppliers
Great Britain

Most of the materials can be bought from large department stores or from any of the following firms:

Beads and sequins

Ells and Farrier Limited
5 Princes Street
London W1R 8PH

John Lewis and Co Ltd
Oxford Street
London W1

Sesame Ventures
Greenham Hall
Wellington
Somerset

Embroidery threads and accessories

Mrs Mary Allen
Turnditch
Derbyshire

Art Needlework Industries Ltd
7 St Michael's Mansions
Ship Street
Oxford

Threads and accessories

Craftsman's Mark Limited
Broadlands
Shortheath
Farnham
Surrey

J Hyslop Bathgate and Company
Victoria Works
Galashiels

Mace and Nairn
89 Crane Street
Salisbury
Wiltshire

The Needlewoman Shop
146 Regent Street
London W1

Christine Riley
53 Barclay Street
Stonehaven
Kincardineshire AB3 2AR

Threads and accessories

Mrs Joan L Trickett
110 Marsden Road
Burnley
Lancashire

Yarns

21 Portland Street
Taunton TA1 1UV
Somerset

Felt

The Felt and Hessian Shop
34 Greville Street
London EC1

95

Suppliers
USA

Most of the materials can be bought from large department stores or from any of the following firms:

Beads

Amar Pearl and Bead Co Inc
19001 Stringway
Long Island City
New York

Hollander Bead and Novelty Corporation
25 West 37th Street
New York
NY 10018

Embroidery threads and accessories

American Crewel Studio
Box 553 Westfield
New Jersey 07091

American Thread Corporation
90 Park Avenue
New York

Appleton Brothers of London
West Main Road
Little Compton
Rhode Island 02837

Threads and accessories

Craft Yarns
PO Box 355
Pawtucket
Rhode Island
02862

F J Fawcett Co
129 South Street
Boston
Massachusetts 02111

Bucky King Embroideries Unlimited
121 South Drive
Pittsburgh
Pennsylvania 15238

Lily Mills
Shelby
North Carolina 28150

The Needle's Point Studio
7013 Duncraig Court
McLean
Virginia 22101

Threads and accessories

Yarncrafts Limited
3146 M Street
North West
Washington DC

96